Whisky: The Recipe Book (2)
Desserts, Cakes & Preserves

First published in 2013
by
Aird Trading (Publishing)
www.scotlandbooks.co.uk

Authors: Lynne Woods & Doug Vickers

ISBN 978-0-9562126-9-6

Whisky - Usquebaugh - Aqua Vitae -The Water of Life

The earliest documented use of whisky is a report from 1405 into the death of an Irish chieftain who had died due to "an excess of aqua vitae" at Christmas. In 1494, aqua vitae is recorded in an entry in the Scottish Exchequer Rolls - enough malt to produce about 500 bottles of whisky had been sent to Friar John Cor on the orders of the King. It is to be hoped that the events of 1494 in Scotland had a happier outcome than those of 1405 in Ireland!

In the intervening years since the 15th century, whisky has been distilled for and enjoyed by royalty and common man alike and is now available in a vast range of brands from Europe, the Americas, India and Japan, in addition to the traditional "Scotch" and "Irish" products.

Throughout the centuries whisky production has seen turbulent times, with illicit stills, tax evasion and smuggling. Nowadays, however, the whisky industry is highly regulated on an international scale. For example, to be called "Scotch", a whisky must not only be distilled in Scotland but must also conform to many other regulations.

Scotch itself can be subdivided into several categories, each with its own set of "rules".
- Single Malt Scotch Whisky - made from malted barley from a single distillery.
- Single Cask Malt Scotch Whisky - bottled from a single cask.
- Vatted (blended) Malt Scotch Whisky - a combination of malt whisky from more than one distillery.
- Blended Scotch Whisky - a combination of a small proportion of single malt whisky blended with a larger quantity of other whiskies.

There are a huge variety of whiskies readily available, each with a taste or character of its own and it would seem that most whisky drinkers have their preferred tipple. Preference normally comes from some experimentation and there is no reason why experimentation should not be taken a stage further by using whisky as an ingredient and not merely as an aperitif or digestive to accompany a meal. This is the aim of this book, along with its sister title "Whisky: The Recipe Book (1) - Starters & Main Courses".

In creating the recipes in this book, several single malts, blended whiskies and liqueur whiskies have been used to provided a range of flavours. However, "Each to his own" - there is no reason why ones own favourite tipple should not be substituted, or even why a non Scotch could not be tried. Also of some importance is quantity - should you feel that a recipe lacks the required "zing", then feel free to "adjust" the quantity the next time around.

And finally ....why not enjoy a glass of your favourite tipple whilst preparing your meal? *"Good Health!"*

Some notes ....

Servings ....

Most recipe books list ingredients sufficient to serve four, or even six, people. Given that it is usually easier to double or triple ingredients than to half them, we have (unless otherwise stated) used quantities which will serve two people.

The imperial/metric dilemma ....

It is not practical to always supply exact conversions between metric and imperial measures, as many amounts do not have "sensible" equivalents. For this reason conversions may vary slightly between recipes, according to which quantities work best. For the best results, use either metric or imperial but do not mix the two!

For liquids, we have used millilitres and fluid ounces in some recipes, whereas in others it has been more practical to use teaspoons and tablespoons. For those using this book who are not familiar with the size of British spoons (and they vary even here!) we have used a teaspoon as 5 millilitres and a tablespoon as 15 millilitres.

Abbreviations used in this book ....

g - gram(s)
oz. - ounce(s)
ml. - millilitre(s)
fl. oz. - fluid ounce(s)
teasp. - teaspoon(s)
tbsp. - tablespoon(s)
'c - degrees centigrade
'f - degrees fahrenheit
cm. - centimetre(s)
" - inch(es)

Whisky tasting notes ....

With each recipe we have included "whisky tasting notes". These are only intended as a guideline and the final choice is, of course, down to personal taste. However, given the differences in the strength of flavour, "smokiness" and "sweetness" between various types of whisky, it would sometimes be wasteful to use an expensive single malt when a blended whisky would give satisfactory results or to use a delicately flavoured whisky which would be lost in the stronger flavours of other ingredients - but, by all means, feel free to experiment!

A gentle word of caution ....

You probably don't need reminding but whisky IS alcoholic. Take care to consume it responsibly. Whisky disguised as trifle or fruit salad still counts as alcohol!

Contents

Desserts

Cakes

Preserves

Miscellaneous

Marmalade Puddings with Whisky & Orange Sauce

Ingredients: (makes six)

For the puddings:

60ml./4 tbsp. whisky
1 tbsp. orange/tangerine marmalade
50g/2 oz. margarine
50g/2 oz. Sugar
125g/5 oz. Self-raising flour
1 egg beaten

For the sauce:

1 tbsp. marmalade
225ml./8 fl. oz. evaporated milk
15 - 30 ml./1 - 2 tblsp. whisky
1 small mandarin orange for decoration

This sauce is so simple to make but absolutely delicious!

Method:

1. Pre-heat the oven to 190'c/375'f/gas 5. Grease 6 individual deep bun tins (or use paper bun cases).
2. Make the puddings: Mix together the whisky and marmalade. Beat together the margarine, sugar, egg, flour and whisky mix. Divide between the bun tins and bake for 15 - 25 minutes until risen and golden.
3. Make the sauce: Heat together the marmalade and evaporated milk. Boil for 2 minutes, stirring, until thickened slightly. Remove from the heat and stir in the whisky.
4. To serve: When the puddings are cooked, turn out. Re-heat the sauce if necessary, serving a little alongside the puddings and the remainder in a jug. Garnish with segments of mandarin orange.

Whisky tasting notes: A blended whisky is fine to give a really lovely flavour to both the puddings and the sauce.

Rhubarb Surprise

Ingredients: (serves two)

200g/8oz. rhubarb washed, trimmed and cut into 1cm./0.5" lengths

2cm./1" piece of fresh ginger peeled & grated

70g/4 level tbsp. light Muscovado sugar

70ml./5 tbsp. whisky

75g/3 oz. stem ginger biscuits crushed

125ml./5 fl. oz. double cream

Method:

1. Put the rhubarb, ginger, sugar & whisky in a saucepan. Heat gently until the sugar has dissolved then cover and simmer gently for 5 minutes. Remove from the heat and allow to cool slightly then strain, reserving the rhubarb and returning the juice to the pan.
2. Boil the juice briskly, stirring frequently, for 3 to 4 minutes until it begins to turn syrupy. Remove the syrup from the heat and allow to cool.
3. Crush the biscuits.
4. Whip the cream until it forms soft peaks.
5. To assemble: Divide the rhubarb, cream and half of the crushed biscuits (reserve the other half - see below) between two glasses as follows: A layer of biscuit in the bottom of each glass, followed by a layer of rhubarb then cream. Add a second layer of rhubarb, then biscuit, then cream. Chill for at least half an hour. Just before serving, sprinkle the remaining biscuit on top and drizzle with the syrup.

Whisky tasting notes: A "sweet" Speyside whisky links the rhubarb and ginger perfectly - with this unusual trio of flavours three is definitely not a crowd!

Whisky Poached Pears

Ingredients: (makes four)

4 pears
1.5 teasp. ground ginger
5 tbsp. golden syrup
175ml./7 fl. oz. whisky
375ml./15 fl. oz. water
To serve: single cream
stem ginger biscuits

If serving cold, this dish can be completely prepared the previous day.

Method:

1. Put the ginger in a small saucepan and gradually add the syrup. Mix thoroughly then blend in the whisky and the water. Heat gently.
2. Leaving the pears whole with the stalks intact, cut a sliver from the bottom so they will stand up and then remove the skins. Place upright in the pan.
3. Simmer gently, basting frequently if not completely covered, until the pears are cooked through but not mushy. Remove the pears from the pan and set aside.
4. Turn up the heat & boil the sauce for 20 - 25 minutes until syrupy.
5. To serve: Either allow to cool completely and serve cold or gently re-heat the pears in the syrup. Serve with single cream & stem ginger biscuits.

Whisky tasting notes: The ginger & syrup give the sauce a lovely rich flavour so a delicate and expensive single malt would perhaps be overpowered. We used a blended whisky for a great result.

Upsidedown Pudding with Whisky Pineapple Custard

Ingredients: (makes four)
100g tin pineapple pieces (juice or syrup)
50ml./3.5 tbsp. whisky liqueur
50g/2 oz. margarine
50g/2 oz. Sugar
1 egg beaten
60g/2.5 oz. Self raising flour
Approx. 160ml./5 fl. oz. evaporated milk
3 teasp. cornflour

You will also need: 4 paper or silicone bun cases.

The custard sauce is really yummy! Any leftovers are equally nice served cold.

Method:

1.Pre-heat the oven to 190'c/375'f/gas 5.

2. Drain the pineapple well, reserving the juice. Put the pineapple in a bowl, pour the whisky over and set aside.

3 To make the sponge: Beat together the margarine, sugar, egg and flour. Arrange a few pieces of drained pineapple in the bottom of each bun case and then divide the sponge mixture between them. Bake for 15 - 20 minutes until golden and cooked through.

4. Drain the pineapple again. Set aside the fruit and add the whisky to the reserved pineapple juice.

5 To make the sauce: Make the whisky and pineapple juice up to 10 fl. oz./0.5 pint with evaporated milk. In a pan, mix the cornflour with a little of this liquid then blend in the remaining evaporated milk mix. Heat gently, stirring, until thickened.

6. When the puddings are cooked, allow to cool slightly before turning out upside down. Reheat the sauce and serve with the puddings, alongside the reserved pineapple pieces.

Whisky tasting notes: Experiment - The choice is yours!

Tangy Whisky & Lemon Cheesecakes

Ingredients: (makes two)
1 lemon scrubbed
150g/6oz. chocolate digestive bicsuits
75g/3oz. butter or margarine
200g/8oz. cream cheese
30ml./2 tbsp. Greek yoghurt
2 rounded teasp. sugar
45 ml./3 tbsp. whisky

You will need two 7cm. ring moulds or individual loose-bottomed flan tins.

Method:

1. Remove a few shavings of lemon skin with a potato peeler then use a sharp knife to cut these into thin strips. Place in hot water to soak. Use a grater to remove the remaining lemon zest before squeezing the lemon. Set aside the lemon juice & zest.
2. Either grease the flan tins or, if using ring moulds, cover a chopping board with cling film or baking parchment, grease this with butter or margarine and place the greased rings on the board.
3. Crush the biscuits into crumbs, either in a food processor or by putting them into a plastic bag and crushing with a rolling pin.
4. Gently melt the butter/margarine and combine with the biscuit crumbs. Divide between the two greased tins/moulds and press in firmly. Place in the fridge to firm while you make the topping.
5. Beat together the cream cheese, yoghurt, sugar, whisky, lemon juice & zest. Adjust whisky & sugar to taste. Pile the mixture on top of the two crumb bases. Chill for 15 minutes in the freezer before gently removing the moulds. Decorate with the strips of lemon zest.

Whisky tasting notes: The choice of whisky is really a matter of taste. As a delicate whisky may well be over-powered by the flavour of the lemon, choose a blended whisky or a strongly flavoured malt.

Whisky Lemon Jelly

Ingredients: (makes two individual jellies)

2 lemons
6 teasp. sugar
1 sachet powdered gelatine
4 tbsp./2 fl. oz. whisky
125 ml./5 fl.oz. double cream

An impressive sweet - prepare the day before and just add the cream when serving.

Method:

1. With a potato peeler, remove the zest from one lemon. Cut into thin strips and just cover with hot water. Set aside.
2. Juice the lemons. Make the juice up to 325ml./10.5 fl. oz. with water.
3. Place the lemon juice & sugar in a saucepan and heat gently. When the sugar has dissolved, sprinkle on the gelatine and stir until dissolved. Do not allow to boil. Remove from the heat, add the whisky and allow to cool for 10 - 15 minutes, stirring frequently.
4. Pour into two individual glasses and place in the fridge. Allow at least four hours to set..
5. Drain the lemon zest and set aside.
6. To serve: Whip the cream into soft peaks, divide between two glasses and top with the drained strips of lemon zest.

Whisky tasting notes: The choice of whisky is really a matter of taste. We used a Speyside single malt for a lovely subtle flavour.

Whisky Orange Delight

You will need two, individual, loose -based flan tins.

Ingredients: (serves two)

For the base:

100g/4oz. gingernuts

50g/2 oz. margarine or butter + extra for greasing

For the filling:

1 satsuma/mandarin orange

60ml./4 tbsp. whisky liqueur

1 orange jelly

1 small tin (200ml.) evaporated milk

Method:

1. Prepare the base: Grease the flan tins. Crush the gingernuts to crumbs. Melt the margarine and combine with the biscuit. Press into the flan bases. Put in the fridge to set.

Make the filling:

2. Using a grater, remove the zest from the orange and place in a bowl. Peel the orange, divide into segments & prick each several times with a skewer. Add these to the bowl with half the liqueur.

3. Put the jelly to dissolve in 100ml./3.5 fl.oz. boiling water.

4. Whip the evaporated milk until thick, creamy and doubled in bulk. Drain the mandarin segments and set aside. Add the liquid to the dissolved jelly, along with the remaining liqueur then fold gently into the evaporated milk. Divide between the prepared bases and chill for 2 - 3 hours until set.

5. To serve: Gently remove the flans from their tins and decorate with the reserved orange segments.

Whisky tasting notes: The combination of flavours in this dessert is superb. Use your favourite whisky liqueur the first time - try a different one next time!

The Ultimate Banana Split

Make the ice cream and chocolate sauce at least six hours in advance.

Ingredients: (makes two)
2 bananas
For the ice cream:
200g/8 oz. vanilla ice cream
40 ml./3 tbs. whisky
For the chocolate sauce:
140 ml./5.5 fl. oz. evaporated milk
110g/4.5 oz. milk or plain chocolate
40 ml./3 tbsp. whisky
To serve: 1 small carton double cream
1 x chocolate flake

This chocolate sauce is simply too good not to also try on pears, sponge puddings etc. (Or for an even greater indulgence simply pour some into a glass and serve as a liqueur!!)

Method:

1. Whisky Ice Cream: Allow the ice cream to soften then beat with 40ml. whisky (or whizz in a food processor). Re-freeze.
2. Chocolate Sauce: Place the evaporated milk in a saucepan with the chocolate. Warm gently until the chocolate has completely melted then simmer gently for 2 - 3 minutes. Add the whisky & allow to cool completely. (It will go nice and gooey.)
3. To assemble: Whip the cream into firm peaks. Split the bananas lengthways. Arrange on individual serving dishes, sandwiched together with scoops of ice cream. Pile on the whipped cream and pour the chocolate sauce around the edges. Pop half a chocolate flake on top to decorate. Enjoy!

Whisky tasting notes: A light, sweet-tasting Speyside malt is ideal - experimenting provides a good excuse to try this again.... and again!

Whisky Jellied Peach Flan

Ingredients: (serves 2 with seconds!)
400g can of tinned peaches
70ml./2.5 fl.oz. whisky
200g/8 oz. puff pastry thawed
beaten egg to brush the pastry
0.5 tbsp. cornflour

Put the peaches to soak overnight if possible!

Method:

1. Drain the peaches well, reserving the juice. Pour the whisky over them and leave to soak for at least 3 - 4 hours but preferably overnight.
2. Pre-heat the oven to 220'c/425'f/gas 7. Lightly grease or line a rectangular baking sheet.
3. Drain the peaches well, reserving the whisky. Roll out the pastry to a rectangle approx. 26cm. X 17cm. Score a line 1.5 cm. from the edge all the way round. Brush the 1.5cm. border with beaten egg then arrange the peach slices inside the border. Bake for 15 - 20 minutes until the edges have risen and turned golden. Allow to cool completely.
4. Put 100ml./4 fl.oz. of the reserved juice in a pan and boil vigorously for 2 - 3 minutes until slightly thickened. Mix the cornflour with a little more of the reserved juice to make a smooth paste then stir into the hot juice. Cook gently for 2 - 3 minutes, stirring, until thickened. Remove from the heat and stir in the whisky.
5. Allow the jelly to cool slightly before spooning/spreading over the peaches. Place the flan in the fridge to set the jelly.

Whisky tasting notes: A really smoky single malt is ideal for this recipe, creating a wonderful harmony with the flavour of the peaches.

Cranachan Plus!

Ingredients: (serves two)

25g/1 oz. rolled oats
20g/0.75 oz. Demerara sugar
25g/1 oz. flaked almonds
125ml./5 fl. oz. double/whipping cream
125g/5 oz. cream cheese
35 - 40 ml./2 - 3 tbsp. whisky
200g/8 oz. raspberries

A traditional Scottish dessert but with added flavour and crunch!

Method:

1. Pre-heat the grill. Mix the oats and sugar in a flameproof dish or on a piece of foil. Place under the grill and toast until golden brown, turning constantly. Set aside.
2. Toast the almonds until golden brown, being careful not to allow them to burn. Set aside.
3. Whip the cream until standing in soft peaks. Set aside.
4. Beat together the cream cheese and whisky.
5. Combine the cheese mixture and cream. Adjust whisky to taste.
6. Reserving a few raspberries for decoration, gently fold in the raspberries, oats and half the toasted almonds.
7. Pile into serving dishes and place in the fridge to chill.
8. Just before serving, sprinkle on the remaining almonds, top with the reserved raspberries and add an extra drizzle of whisky if required.

Whisky tasting notes: Again, a matter of taste! Why not try a blended whisky in the main dish and a single malt for the final drizzle - perhaps a fruity Highland?

Whisky Chocolate Ice Cream with White Chocolate Sauce

Ingredients: (serves two)

For the ice cream:

100ml./4 fl.oz. double cream

2 eggs beaten

200ml./8 fl. oz. milk

50g/2 oz. Demerara sugar

75g/3 oz. milk or plain chocolate

45ml./3 tbsp. whisky

For the sauce:

100g/4 oz. white chocolate

160ml./5.5 fl.oz. evaporated milk

1 teasp. vanilla essence

60ml./2 fl.oz. milk

To serve: a selection of ice cream wafers

This is a truly decadent dessert!

Method:

1. Put the cream, eggs, milk & sugar in a pan. Heat gently (don't boil or the eggs will scramble!) for 5 - 6 minutes until thickened. Remove from the heat and break the chocolate into the pan. Stir until dissolved then add the whisky. Put in a plastic container and freeze for half an hour. Remove from the freezer, stir & return to the freezer until completely set - this will take several hours.

2. Make the sauce: Heat all the ingredients together gently until the chocolate is completely dissolved then boil vigorously for 2 - 3 minutes until the mixture begins to thicken. Remove from the heat and cool.

3. To serve: Remove the ice cream from the freezer and allow to soften slightly. Serve scoops of ice cream with wafers & small, individual pots of the sauce. Enjoy!

Whisky tasting notes: Whisky & chocolate, even with a blended whisky, is a marriage made in Heaven!

Hole-In-The-Middle Pudding

Ingredients: (serves two)
150g/6 oz. dried, sliced fruit such as apples, bananas & apricots
125ml./5 fl.oz. whisky

For the sponge:
100g/4 oz. margarine
100g/4 oz. sugar
100g/4 oz. self raising flour
2 eggs beaten

For the icing:
1 tbsp. apple juice
175g/7 oz. icing sugar

For the syrup:
1 tbsp. golden syrup

Method:

1. Place the fruit in a shallow bowl. Cover with the whisky and leave to soak.

2. Preheat the oven to 180'c/350'f/gas 4. Grease or line a 19cm./7" baking tin. Beat together the margarine, sugar, eggs and flour. Bake for 25 - 35 minutes until golden. Turn out and leave to cool slightly. Using a sharp knife or pastry cutter, remove a 9cm./3.5 " circle from the middle.

3. Drain the fruit, reserving the liquid.

4. Make the icing: Mix the apple juice with 1 tbsp. of the reserved liquid. Add the icing sugar slowly to make a smooth, stiff (but spreadable) paste and ice both pieces of cake. Decorate with a few pieces of the drained fruit. Leave to set.

5. Make the syrup: In a pan, combine the remaining liquid from the drained fruit with the golden syrup. Boil vigorously for about 3 minutes until syrupy and rich brown.

6. To serve: Immediately before serving, pile the drained fruit into the hole, drizzle over the syrup then top with the circle of cake.

Whisky tasting notes: The combination of whisky and apple juice makes an unusual icing. We used a blended whisky.

Whisky Crème Brûlée

Ingredients: (makes 4 small or 2 larger)
For the crèmes: 3 egg yolks
3 teasp. caster sugar
250ml./9 fl.oz. double cream
6 drops vanilla essence
15ml./1 tbsp. whisky
For the topping: 10ml./2 teasp. whisky
3 teasp. Demerara sugar
grapes to decorate
You will need: flameproof ramekin dishes

Prepare the day before for easy but impressive entertaining!

Method:

1. Make the crème: Beat the egg yolks & caster sugar together until pale, thick and creamy.

2. Heat the cream in a saucepan until boiling then remove from the heat and add the vanilla essence & 15ml. of whisky before slowly adding to the egg, stirring continuously. Return to the pan and heat gently (do not boil or the egg will scramble!) for 1 - 1.5 minutes until thickened. Pour into the ramekin dishes and place in the fridge to set.

3. To finish: Pre-heat the grill. Mix 2 teasp. whisky with the Demerara sugar. Spread gently over the crèmes and flash under the grill for 1 to 1.5 minutes until motlen & glassy. NB: Take care not to leave unattended - the topping will shoot small flames. Cool slightly then place in the fridge for 2 - 3 hours to set if you want a hard topping, eat sooner for a softer topping.

Whisky tasting notes: A light Speyside, or a crisp, fresh Highland single malt, provides just the strength of flavour with the delicate hint of vanilla in this dessert.

Pineapple Fiesta with Mandarin & Grape Sauce

Ingredients: (serves two)
300g tin mandarins in syrup
70ml./2.25 fl.oz. whisky
6 red or green (or mixed) grapes
half a small, ripe pineapple
lemon juice for brushing
250ml./10 fl.oz. double cream
1 level teasp. cornflour

This exotic dessert is well worth the effort. Although a little fiddly, it is really quite simple to make and looks stunning.

Method:

1. Drain the mandarins, reserving the juice. Put the mandarins into a bowl and pour over 35ml. of the whisky. Wash and halve the grapes. Add to the bowl.

2. Cut the pineapple in half lengthways, including the foliage. Use a sharp knife to cut the inside into cubes and remove, leaving the shell intact, as shown in the picture. Add the pineapple cubes to the bowl of fruit along with any juice from the shell & the remaining whisky. Brush the inside of the shell with lemon juice.

3. Whip the cream until standing in stiff peaks.

4. Strain the fruit & set aside. Make the whisky/juice up to 150ml./6fl.oz. with some of the reserved mandarin juice. Set aside.

5. Puree half of the fruit in a processor or with a hand mixer. Fold half of this mix into the whipped cream and place in the fridge to firm.

C'td....

Pineapple Fiesta (C'td)

6. Make the sauce: Mix the cornflour with a little of the reserved pureed fruit then blend with the reserved whisky/juice. Transfer to a pan, bring to the boil, stirring and remove from the heat when thickened. Allow to cool and transfer to a serving jug.

7. To assemble: Pile two thirds of the fruit into the pineapple shell. Top with the cream mix and the remaining fruit. Serve alongside the sauce and with any left over cream in a separate serving bowl.

Whisky tasting notes: Either a blended or malt whisky adds the necessary "something extra" to both the cream centre of this dessert and the accompanying sauce.

Luxurious Fresh Fruit Salad

Ingredients: (serves two)

1 small peach
1 plum
2 mandarin oranges or clementines
10 red or green grapes
Juice of half a lemon
0.5 teasp. sugar
30 ml./2 tbsp. whisky liqueur

Method:

1. Slice the fruit and chop into bite sized pieces. Cut the grapes in half. Place in a serving bowl.
2. Warm together the lemon juice, sugar, whisky liqueur and 40 ml./8 teasp. water. Do not boil. Allow to cool slightly then pour over the fruit while still warm. Stir then set aside for at least an hour, stirring occasionally. Serve on its own or with fresh cream.

Whisky tasting notes: A splash of liqueur adds a touch of luxury to an ordinary fruit salad.

Honey & Whisky Clementines Topped with Toasted Almonds

Ingredients: (serves two)
6 small clementines (or mandarin oranges)
60ml./2 fl. oz. whisky liqueur
35g/1.25 oz. flaked almonds
60ml./4 tbsp. clear, runny honey
single cream to serve

Our friend, Mel, says the crunch of the topping & the blend of flavours is scrummy!

Method:

1. Peel the clementines or mandarins, removing all the white pith. Prick each several times with a skewer and place in a bowl. Pour over the whisky liqueur and leave to soak for at least an hour, turning over frequently.
2. Arrange the almonds on a sheet of foil on a grill pan and toast briefly under a hot grill until golden brown. NB: Do not leave unattended as these will quickly burn.
3. Drain the oranges, reserving the liqueur, and place in a serving bowl. Combine the liqueur with the honey and pour over the fruit. Sprinkle the toasted almonds over the oranges and serve with a jug of single cream.

Whisky tasting notes: There are several lovely whisky liqueurs readily available in the shops - try ringing the changes & see which is your favourite.

Whisky Lovers' Dream Trifle

Ingredients: (serves two)
200g tin pineapple pieces (in juice or syrup)
100g/4 oz. sponge cake
50ml./3.5 tbsp. whisky
250ml./10fl.oz. thick custard (made up)
175 ml./7 fl. oz. double/whipping cream

This whisky version of an enduringly popular British dessert, ie. sherry trifle, is a real winner which will please all trifle lovers and whisky lovers alike!

Method:

1. If using custard powder, make up and leave to cool.
2. Drain the pineapple, reserving the juice and a few pieces of pineapple for decoration.
3. Break the cake into a serving dish, scatter the fruit on top.
4. Mix the whisky with 70 ml./5 tbsp. of the pineapple juice. Pour over the cake and pineapple. Cover with the custard. (If using custard made from custard powder, let it cool first.)
5. Whisk the cream until standing in stiff peaks then spoon onto the top of the trifle. Decorate with the reserved pineapple pieces.

Whisky tasting notes: Experiment! The choice is yours - a wonderful excuse to try this recipe more than once!

Cherry Cream Meringues with a Whisky Cherry Sauce

Ingredients: (makes four)
4 meringue nests
350g/jar/tin Morello or black cherries in syrup
45ml./1.5 fl.oz. whisky
1 teasp. sugar
1 teasp. cornflour

This recipe works equally well with tinned strawberries.

As the cherries, even in syrup, can taste quite tart, you may need to add a little extra sugar at stages 3 and 4.

Method:

1. Drain the cherries, reserving the juice and a few cherries for decoration.
2. Whip the cream to soft peaks.
3. Either finely chop the cherries or blitz them in a food processor. Add the sugar and 20ml./0.75 fl.oz. of the whisky. Adjust sugar to taste. Gently fold the mix into the cream and place in the fridge to firm.
4. Make the sauce: Place 150ml./5 fl.oz. of the reserved juice in a pan. Blend the cornflour with a little of the juice and then combine with the juice in the pan. Bring to the boil, stirring, then simmer gently for about a minute until syrupy. Remove from the heat, add the remaining whisky and a little sugar if required. Allow to cool.
5. To assemble: Pile the cherry cream into the meringue nests, decorate with the reserved cherries and serve with individual pots of the sauce.

Whisky tasting notes: A blended whisky is fine but, as ever, the choice is yours! Try your favourite single malt - or for a really sweet treat use a whisky liqueur.

Boozy Flapjacks

Ingredients: (makes 12)
75g/3 oz. mixed dried fruit
60 ml./4 tbsp. whisky
75g/3 oz. butter or margarine
100g/4 oz. Demerara sugar
2 level tbsp. golden syrup
175g/7 oz. rolled oats

Soak the fruit overnight for a stronger flavour!

Method:

1. Soak the fruit in the whisky for at least an hour.
2. Preheat the oven to 180'c/350'f/gas 4.
3. Grease a rectangular baking tin (approx. 25cm. X 18cm./10" X 7").
4. In a pan, gently melt together the butter/margarine, sugar & syrup until the sugar has dissolved. Do not allow to boil.
5. Remove from the heat, stir in the whisky and fruit then the oats.
6. Press the mixture into the baking tin and bake for 30 - 40 minutes until golden brown.
7. Allow to cool slightly, run a knife round the edge of the tin then cut into squares but leave in the tin to cool completely before removing.

Whisky tasting notes: We recommend a strongly flavoured whisky - A smoky single malt gives ordinary flapjacks a definite "kick"!

Bran & Whisky Tea Loaf

Ingredients: (makes one loaf)

100g/4oz. bran
125g/5 oz. sugar
250g/10 oz. dried mixed fruit
125ml./5 fl.oz. whisky
125ml./5 fl.oz. milk
125g/5 oz. self raising flour

Serve on its own or smothered in butter! Nice at tea-time or served cut into small cubes with after-dinner coffee.

Method:

1. Place the bran, sugar & fruit in a bowl. Add the milk and whisky. Stir well & leave to soak for at least an hour (but overnight is better).
2. Pre-heat the oven to 180'c/350'f/gas 4. Grease or line a 1 lb. loaf tin.
3. Stir the flour into the fruit mix. Add a little extra flour if the mix is too runny. (It should be slightly stiffer than a "dropping consistency".) Spoon into the prepared tin and bake for an hour to an hour and a half until cooked through. (An inserted skewer should come out clean.)

Whisky tasting notes: A blended or peaty whisky, according to personal preference, is recommended.

Whisky Crust Cake

Ingredients: (makes one cake)
For the cake: 50g/2oz. margarine
50g/2 oz. granulated or caster sugar
65g/2.5 oz. self raising flour
2 eggs beaten
For the topping: 1.25g/5 oz. Demerara sugar
2 fl. oz./4 tbsp. whisky

The scrumptious crunchy topping turns an ordinary sponge cake into something really special!

Method:

1. Pre-heat the oven to 180'c/350'f/gas 4.
Grease or line a 1 lb. loaf tin.

2. Make the sponge: Cream together the margarine and white sugar, add a little flour, then the egg, then the remaining flour (or whizz together all the cake ingredients in a food processor). Spocn into the loaf tin and level the surface. Bake for 30 - 45 minutes until a skewer inserted into the middle of the cake comes away clean. Allow to cool. Do not remove from the tin.

3. Make the topping: In a pan, dissolve the Demerara sugar in the whisky. Bring to the boil & bubble for 2 minutes, stirring continuously, until just beginning to go syrupy. Remove from the heat, allow to cool slightly and then pour over the cake (still in the tin). Allow to cool completely before removing from the tin.

Whisky tasting notes: The choice of whisky is up to the cook! We used a light Speyside whisky which perfectly complimented the flavour of the sponge.

Plum & Whisky Jam

Ingredients:

(makes 2 x 200g/8 oz. jars)
500g/20 oz. plums
400g/16 oz. preserving sugar
35 ml./1.5 tbsp. whisky

Method:

1. Wash the plums & remove stalks. Cut a large cross in the base of each. Cover with boiling water and leave for 5 minutes.
2. Place the sugar in an ovenproof bowl and either microwave on three quarters power for 3 - 4 minutes (stirring frequently to prevent burning) or place in the oven at 170'c/325'f/gas 3 for 10 minutes.
3. Put a small plate in the freezer.
4. Drain the plums and peel. (The skins will now separate easily from the flesh.) Chop roughly, discarding the stones. Place in a heavy based pan along with any juice from chopping and warm gently until the juices start running. Tip in the warmed sugar and continue heating gently until the sugar has completely dissolved then boil rapidly for 10 minutes.
5. Put a small amount of the jam on the pre- cooled plate & push gently with the back of a spoon. If the jam wrinkles it has reached setting point. If not continue to boil for a further few minutes and test again. When setting point has been achieved, allow to cool for 5 minutes, stirring occasionally before adding the whisky. Allow to cool for a further 10 minutes before pouring into clean jars.

Whisky tasting notes: This recipe can be tailored to your own particular taste in whisky - we used a blended whisky and it was delicious.

Rhubarb, Ginger & Whisky Preserve

Ingredients: (makes two x 200g/8 oz. Jars)
350g/14 oz. rhubarb
340g/13.5 oz. preserving sugar
5 - 7cm./2" - 3" piece fresh ginger peeled & grated
35 ml./1.5fl. oz. whisky

Delicious on scones, bread or toast but why stop there? For a really scrumptious stir fry sauce mix equal quantities of the preserve with soy sauce and add to stir fried vegetables or meat just before serving.

Method:

1. Place a small plate in the freezer.
2. Wash and trim the rhubarb into 2.5 cm./1" lengths. Put in a heavy-based pan with the sugar and ginger. Warm gently to dissolve the sugar then boil rapidly for 7 - 10 minutes.
3. Put a small amount on the pre- cooled plate & push gently with the back of a spoon. If the jam wrinkles it has reached setting point. If not continue to boil for a further few minutes and test again.
4. When setting point has been achieved, allow to cool slightly before stirring in the whisky. Allow to cool further (but not set!) before transferring into clean jars.

Whisky tasting notes: A really smoky malt whisky adds a wonderful zing to the rhubarb and ginger flavours in this luxurious preserve.

Petit Fours

Ingredients: (makes 48)
75g/3 oz. white chocolate
75g/3 oz. milk or plain chocolate
170g/6.5 oz. butter or margarine
40ml./8 teasp. whisky liqueur
40ml./8 teasp. a different whisky liqueur
450g/18 oz. icing sugar
chocolate cake decorations

You will also need:
petit four cases, greaseproof paper & a baking tin approx. 17cm./7" square.

Method:

1. Lightly grease the baking tin then arrange a sheet of greaseproof paper in it with a pleat in the middle to divide the tin into two halves.
2. In two separate bowls, either over pans of hot water or in a microwave, melt the chocolate.
3. In a similar way, melt the butter then divide between the two bowls of chocolate. Give each bowl a good stir and then add one liqueur to one bowl and the other liqueur to the second bowl. Beat 225g/9 oz. icing sugar into each mix to make a really stiff mix. Press the two fudge mixes into the two halves of the baking tin and put in the fridge to chill for an hour.
4. Remove from the fridge, mark into squares and add the decorations. Return to the fridge until completely set.
5. When completely set, use a sharp knife to cut the fudge into bite-sized squares. Place each in a petit four case.

NB: STORE IN THE FRIDGE.

Whisky tasting notes: These easy-to-make chocolate treats provide a really professional looking finale to a special meal! Use your favourite whisky liqueurs.

Tipsy Lemonade

Ingredients: (makes two)

1 medium lemon   1.5 tbsp. sugar (or to taste)

250ml./10 fl. oz. boiling water

30ml./1 fl. oz. whisky

Sliced lemon to decorate

Method:

1. Zest & juice the lemon. Put both in a jug with the sugar. Add the boiling water, stir, adjust sugar to taste and leave to cool. When cool, strain and stir in the whisky to taste.
2. Reheat gently, without boiling, to serve hot.

Serve cold for a refreshing summer drink - or drink hot for a winter warmer!

Whisky tasting notes: Blended whisky or single malt? You choose!

Warm Orange Chocolate

Ingredients: (makes two)

90g/3.5 oz. drinking chocolate

300ml./10 fl. oz. pure orange juice

150ml./5 fl.oz. double cream

70ml./2.5 fl. oz. whisky

An indulgent & soothing drink for when the occasion demands.

Method:

1. Dissolve the drinking chocolate in 100ml./3.5 fl.oz. boiling water.
2. Set aside two teasp. cream. Put the rest in a pan with the orange juice, dissolved drinking chocolate & whisky. Heat gently without allowing to boil. Pour into serving glasses and swirl the remaining cream on top. NB: When pouring hot liquid into glass, place a teaspoon in the container while you pour to avoid cracking the glass.

Whisky tasting notes: We used a blended whisky which tasted great. If using a single malt adjust whisky to taste - use less or more!

Florentines

Ingredients: (makes 30)
For the tops:
25g/1 oz. margarine
75g/3 oz. Demerara sugar
1 teasp. golden syrup
90ml./3 fl. oz. double cream
1 teasp. whisky
25g/1 oz. self raising flour
extra margarine for greasing
50g/1.75 oz. whole almonds
50g/1.75 oz. whole hazelnuts
25g/1 oz. flaked almonds
75g/2.5 oz. mixed dried fruit
For the bases:
75g/2.5 oz. plain chocolate
75g/2.5 oz. white chocolate
20g/0.75 oz. margarine
4 teasp. whisky
greaseproof paper/baking parchment

Method:

1. Pre-heat the oven to 200'c/400'f/gas 6. Line two flat baking sheets with greaseproof paper or baking parchment and grease with some melted margarine.

2. Make the tops: Melt the margarine, syrup & sugar together in a saucepan. Add the cream and heat gently for 2 - 3 minutes (do not boil) until the sugar has dissolved. Remove from the heat, stir in the whisky then add the fruit and nuts. Allow to cool for 10 minutes then drop teaspoonfuls of the mixture onto the prepared baking sheet, well spaced and spreading the mixture into circles. Bake for 12 - 15 minutes until golden. Remove from the oven and leave to cool until set enough to handle before peeling off the paper and placing upside down on a fresh sheet of paper.

3. For the bases: Melt together the plain chocolate and 10g of margarine. Remove from the heat and stir in 2 teasp. whisky. Allow to cool until thick but still spreadable. Spread a layer of chocolate on each of half of the upturned tops. Repeat with the white chocolate & remaining florentines. Leave to set completely. Store in an airtight container, separating the florentines from each other with layers of greaseproof paper or baking parchment.

Whisky tasting notes: A peaty single malt, or a sharp Highland whisky, gives these lovely gooey treats something extra special.

Whisky Chocolate Grapes

Ingredients:

75g/3 oz. milk or plain chocolate
30ml./1 fl.oz. whisky
20 - 25 grapes rinsed & dried
You will also need: approx. 50 cocktail sticks
1 large potato

Simple to make, these really are a delight. Use as an alternative to after-dinner mints. Why not also try with cherries, pineapple cubes or even fresh strawberries?

Method:

1. Break the chocolate into a pan.
2. Add the whisky to the pan and warm gently until the chocolate is completely melted. Do not allow to boil.
3. Remove the pan from the heat and allow the chocolate to cool slightly.
4. Cut the potato in half lengthways.
5. Spear the grapes on cocktail sticks (end-on, like lollipops) and dip into the chocolate to completely coat. Push the ends of the cocktail sticks into the potatoes to drip. Leave until the chocolate has completely set.
6. To serve: Carefully remove the cocktail sticks. Discard the potato. Place the chocolate grapes in a serving dish with clean cocktail sticks for "spearing".

Store in an airtight container.

Whisky tasting notes: A blended whisky is fine but, as ever, the choice is yours! Try your favourite single malt - or for a really sweet treat use a whisky liqueur.

RECIPE BOOKS IN THIS SERIES

COLLECTIONS OF DELICIOUS RECIPES USING INGREDIENTS IN IMAGINATIVE WAYS......

- Clear layout
- Easy to follow recipes
- Step by step instructions
- Clear ingredient lists

HAGGIS:
THE RECIPE BOOK

ISBN: 978-0-9562126-4-1

Recipes for all occasions

WHISKY:
THE RECIPE BOOK (1)
STARTERS & MAIN COURSES

ISBN: 978-0-9562126-8-9

Refreshingly different

WHISKY:
THE RECIPE BOOK (2)
DESSERTS, CAKES & PRESERVES

ISBN: 978-0-9562126-9-6

Helpful hints & tips

Aird Trading (Publishing)
Tel: 07889 700420
email:schoolhouse.aird@btinternet.com
www.scotlandbooks.co.uk